EXPERIENCING THE SPIRIT

MY JOURNEY WITH CHRIST

DOUGLAS BABCOCK

Copyright © 2022 Douglas Babcock

Published by CaryPress International Books
www.CaryPress.com

All rights reserved. No part of this publication may be reproduced, distributed, or transmitted in any form or by any means, including photocopying, recording, or other electronic or mechanical methods, without the prior written permission of the publisher, except in the case of brief quotations embodied in critical reviews and certain other noncommercial uses permitted by copyright law.

CONTENTS

Dedication and Thanks v

Introduction 1
Conversations with God 7
Love 15
Forgiveness 23
Listening to Christ 31
Calling the Apostles 41
Peace with Death 47
The Kingdom 53
The Ministry 59
Jesus and the Ten Commandments 69
The Blessing of Adversity 75
The Illusion of Control 81
The Lord's Handmaid 87
Embracing the Cross 93
The Prodigal Son 99
The Love of Christ 105
Finding Christ 121

DEDICATION AND THANKS

This book is dedicated to anyone willing to trust that God actively works in their lives. And I pray that you bring His message of love, mercy, joy, and peace to everyone. Leave anyone you meet better off for having encountered you.

I would like to thank God for inspiring me to put my thoughts in writing. I live in Your mercy and love now and always.

I would like to thank Dr. James Baxendale, Ph.D., for reading every word of this text with me and sharing his thoughts, ideas, and encouragement. I am so grateful that God put you into my life. I pray you have a happy and restful retirement.

I want to thank my mother for her continued support of my music, photography, and writing. I love you, I love you, I love you.

I want to thank my wife, Carrie, for her support in all my creative ventures. I love you.

God, let me not pray to be sheltered from life's dangers, obstacles, or challenges,
But to be fearless in facing them.
Lord, let me not beg for the stilling of my pain or discomfort,
But for the heart to conquer it.
Father, let me not look for allies on life's battlefield,
But to Your guidance alone.
God, let me not crave in anxious fear to be saved,
But to trust in your infinite mercy.

Douglas Babcock
Circa 2000

INTRODUCTION

Our house has a large window in the bathroom that faces east. Even on overcast days, light streams into the room. On clear days, the sunrises are spectacular as the yellow rays of light flicker through the branches and leaves of the tree just outside the window. It really is magical.

My wife places a fresh bouquet on the sill of this window about once every week. They're placed in their vase, they live, they die, and the whole cycle begins again. As with the tree outside the window, the flowers catch the sunlight and cast yellows, pinks, and reds throughout the room. It is so pleasant that I often linger there, watching the colors as I prepare for the day. And I whisper "thank you" to God for sharing that experience with me.

These are simple things. And I am learning to appreciate the simple things in my life. I would largely have to credit the pandemic for this. I believe it made many people slow down and see some of the things they'd been missing. Children were home with moms and dads, and we all had to find a new normal with our Chromebooks and Zoom Meetings. Something that worked for everyone. Some families flourished while others struggled. For me, it meant slowing down and finding joy in the little things happening in my life.

While we all experience a large event on occasion, our lives are mostly knit together with simple things. The smell of a flower. A kiss I share with my wife. Hearing my daughter sing while baking in the kitchen. Listening to my son playing guitar through his bedroom door. We need to slow down, so we are present enough to *experience* these moments.

What does a rose smell like? What did that kiss feel like? We don't have words in our language that can accurately describe such things. The only way to know them is to *experience* them. And this is how we must also experience Christ; slowing down to His pace and finally being quiet and still long enough to hear His voice. This isn't so easy to do. Our world pulls us seemingly in every direction at once. And it does so at a dizzying pace. The notion of slowing down can appear insane.

So, how can we experience Christ unless we slow down and seek a relationship with Him? The answer is obvious. We cannot. Christ will always be there for us. He promised that[1]. But as with any relationship, this is a two-way street. We need to do our part.

Christ invites us into His life daily. "I stand at the door and knock…[2]" Responding to that knocking and opening that door will change you forever, so be prepared. You cannot experience Christ and not be changed. When I decided to answer that knocking, I started learning how to be still. "Be still and know that I am God[3]." I started listening and

---

[1] Matthew 28:20
[2] Revelation 3:20
[3] Psalm 46:10

trusting that He was doing His work in me, even when I couldn't feel a thing. He was changing me. Calling me. He wants me to be a perfect reflection of His love to everyone I meet. This means people we like, and people we do not like.

Praying for people we like is easy. Praying for someone we despise?[4] Why would we even bother? Perhaps we have been deeply hurt by someone, and praying for them is the last thing we want to do. And if we can muster the strength to pray for them, our prayers have a hollow feeling, a lack of sincerity.

But that's OK. In my experience, if continued, our prayers take root and become more genuine. This is love. This is performing God's work.

"I love you." "I love you too." How many times have we had this conversation with someone we love? How many more times will we have this same conversation? Probably a lot. I am not suggesting that our brief love conversations

---

[4] Matthew 5:43-48

are not authentic. But if we are honest about it, sometimes they become routine. Sometimes we recite them without thinking about what we are saying. Sometimes I see the flowers my wife places in our window and experience nothing. But it does not mean that Christ is not present, calling me to experience Him. He's there, and if I experience nothing, it's my fault, not His.

So how do we experience Christ? All I can do is share my own experiences and hope that you find them useful. That's what this book is about. How to experience Christ.

Before we go any further, I want to make clear that I am not a theologian or expert in anything spiritual or religious. I'm just a guy who seeks to experience Christ in the simple things that happen moment by moment. I am still learning and don't always hear Christ speaking to me. But I am open and ready to listen. And that's all you must do too.

Doug
May 2022

CONVERSATIONS WITH GOD

Growing up, I wasn't exposed to religion or spirituality, certainly not on a regular basis. I was taught to pray for my family and friends before bed, but I do not remember anything much beyond that. Even so, this planted the tiny seed[5] that would eventually sprout and grow in later years.

When I review my life, there are certainly many times that I experienced Christ working in my life but did not know it. At least not at the time. I was too interested in baseball, music, and girls to give much notice to God. Now that I

---

[5] Luke 13:19

am older, I can say with great certainty that God was actively working in my life.

I learned how to play the saxophone and guitar at a young age and continue playing to this day. In fact, I've been playing a guitar/vocal solo act in various venues for the past ten or so years. God has graciously given me the experience on many occasions of someone coming to me and saying, "I haven't heard that song in 30 years! Thank you so much!" This is an experience of which I never grow tired.

Well, my father moved into an assisted living facility about two years ago. When he did, he offered me all his photography gear that included a rather nice digital camera and a couple of lenses. As with most things in my life, I jumped into photography with both feet. I started taking nature photos, family pics, etc. and found that I had a reasonably good eye for composition. I've upgraded the camera and lenses twice since then and now have a sole proprietor business that makes me a "real" photographer. It is truly a joy. So much so, that I considered dropping out of the music scene altogether to pursue photography.

Figuring that I would now be taking photographs as my main creative activity, I sold all my live music gear, including a rather nice PA system and monitor. My guitar sat untouched as the days passed and the dust grew deeper on the outside of its case.

I always found it difficult to have so many interests, each one vying for my attention. If I played my saxophone, my guitar was not being used. When I played my guitar, my camera was not being used. And so it went, frustrating me that I hadn't the time or energy to pursue them all. I should point out here that I am somewhat of a perfectionist, so not only did I want to do these things, but I wanted to do them well. Perfectly, in fact. I saw this as an impossible task knowing that each activity required time and effort. I had to give up something to alleviate my anxiety. So, the guitar and singing would have to move into the background. The COVID-19 pandemic put the kibosh on all live music anyway, which made my choice appear even more sensible.

But as we started coming out of COVID-19, live music started to slowly come back into the venues around town.

But I would have no part in it. Or so I thought. Bear in mind that I sincerely believed this is what God wanted. But God has His own way of speaking to us. Let me tell you what He said to me and how I experienced His word.

I was taking photographs of sunflowers at a local park. It was a clear day and I've always enjoyed the bees and butterflies that attend to the sunflowers. I couldn't wait to get home and upload my photos to my computer and review them. But on the way back to my truck, I ran into a woman who served at one of the venues where I used to play. "Where have you been?" she asked. "You really should contact the music director and get back in the rotation. We would love to have you back!" Little did I realize that God had started a conversation with me.

My son works at a local barbeque restaurant. He does everything from washing dishes to serving tables and he seems to enjoy the work. Well, he sent me a text one evening while he was still at work indicating that live music was coming back to the restaurant on Friday nights. Now, Colin's taste in music and my taste in music are polar opposites and it made me wonder if he had sent the text to me by mistake. So, when I saw him the next day, I asked him about it. He assured me that he sent it on purpose and that he thought my musical repertoire would be a good fit. Interesting that God would use a text to speak to me.

Flat Rock, NC is one of my favorite places to visit and my wife and I plan to retire there at some point. We are quite interested in some of the tiny home communities in that area. There are trails galore for hiking (yet another passion of mine) and lots of content for photography. We had just arrived at our hotel room when my phone rang. It was one of the Wake County Career and Education Librarians named Celia. Most people are not aware, but the libraries in Wake County have a robust music program where musicians of all styles are invited to come in and play. I have been fortunate enough to have been invited many times. Well, she was calling to see if I would be willing to come back and play soon.

It was at this moment that I fully understood that God was speaking to me. I hadn't had three separate experiences with God, it was just one long conversation. It just took me a little while to understand what He wanted. So, I accepted Celia's invitation to play and knew that I would have to start playing again. Soon. Anyone who has played a steel-stringed guitar knows how merciless they can be on the fingertips, and I hadn't played my guitar for a while. This was going to hurt.

So, I played, and I hurt, and I played, and I hurt, and at some point, I stopped hurting and things started coming together again. I bought a nice little combo amp to replace the systems I had sold, and I was "gig-ready." And because I now believe so deeply that God wants me to sing and play, I do so nearly every day. And I haven't enjoyed playing this much ever.

This "conversation" with God lasted several months before I got the message. But I know much better now how to listen to God. It takes great patience and prayer. And it takes a willingness to change course if that's what's required. "In all my ways acknowledge Him, and He will direct my paths."[6] Very true.

And so, what this experience has taught me is that God does communicate His desires, often through other people. And His idea of time is way different than mine. I'm no different than the next person; I want the things I want, and I want them now. But that's not the way it goes. If we really want to communicate with God, we must be quiet, still, patient, and reflective. And it's been my experience that, if we earnestly do these things, we will hear what He is saying to us.

---

[6] Proverbs 3:6

LOVE

A friend of mine once said, "I cannot hear a word you are saying because your actions are so loud." Talk is cheap, or at least it can be. It's very easy to say, "I love you." I say these very words often, and I mean what I say.

But my words must be supported by what I do. In fact, my words are completely meaningless without action. Am I patient with someone who is trying me to my very core? Am I kind when confronted with rudeness and selfishness? No, not always. There are times when I return rudeness with rudeness and selfishness with selfishness. But all that does is make more rudeness and selfishness in the world. Not love.

Love has not been so beautifully described anywhere as in Paul's letter to the Corinthians[7]. His description of Love is complete and simple. Be patient. Be kind. Don't hold a grudge. Forgive all wrongs. I have read this passage countless times and I get something new from it with each reading; such is its brilliance. It is often read during marriage ceremonies to highlight love as the main staple of a successful Christian marriage. But we must get past the bridal gowns and tuxedos to really understand what Paul means.

To avoid any confusion, I should point out that I use the New Living Translation (NLT) and The Revised New Jerusalem versions of the bible in my studies. There are certain translations, including the Standard King James Version (KJV), that use "charity" in place of "love" in Paul's first letter to the Corinthians. Merriam-Webster defines charity as "benevolent goodwill toward or **love** of humanity." I trust this will not be a sticking point for anyone.

---

[7] 1 Corinthians 13:1-13

Paul means undiscriminating love. Undiscriminating love includes everyone. We love them through our patience with them, even when they are intolerable. We love them through our kindness to them, even when they don't deserve it. We love them by not being rude, even when they are rude to us. We love them by not storing up grievances, but by forgiving them. For everything. We love them by making allowances, by trusting, and by enduring whatever comes our way. We are instructed to love everyone at every moment.

This sounds impossible. But nothing is impossible with God[8]. Let me say that again. Nothing is impossible with God. We are limited and struggle to love without discrimination. But God is not limited, and He does not struggle to love. God is love. And He wants us to experience His love every day and at every moment. He is constantly calling to us, sharing Himself with us, showing us the way. And once you experience that kind of love, you will be changed forever. You will look for ways to

---

[8] Matthew 19:26

experience God and His love. You will slow down, be still, and wait. And if you do this with anticipation, you will experience God's love for you.

During the sermon on the mount[9], Jesus tells us to love our enemies and even to pray for them (Matthew 5:43-48). But is this something we do? Do we hold on to resentments? I can say with vast experience that holding onto resentments hurts nobody except the one holding the resentments. It is not unlike keeping a prisoner behind bars. You must feed them and provide a certain level of care. This is the cost of keeping someone locked up, even if only in our minds. We remind ourselves of such resentments, and we hold tightly to them every day. Do this long enough and our resentments will grow into something of our own making, something completely different than reality. I have done this more times than I care to admit. But Jesus shows us the way out of this misery. Pray for them. By doing so, we are practicing love at its highest level.

---

[9] Matthew 5: 1-29

Several years ago, I made a list of people with whom I had resentments. The list was much longer than I anticipated. It included family members, coworkers, and friends. I was mad at everyone. In my mind, these people had hurt me and deserved my anger. I relived these resentments as I wrote them on paper. But afterward, I began to see my part in these resentments. Some of them looked so ridiculous on paper that I laughed at them and they instantly evaporated. Others still hurt deeply. What was the answer? Love them with prayer.

So, I began praying for them. At first, my prayers were not heartfelt. But as I continued down this path, these resentments that had weighed so heavily on me over the years began to disappear. My prayers became more sincere as I asked God to give them blessings. I no longer had to keep them locked away in my prison of resentments. Love was the key that opened the doors. Over time, I lost my anger and saw my part in all of this. I had held on to those resentments so tightly.

When we love the way God asks us to love, we experience His love for us. When we pray for those who have offended us, God is pleased with us. He is pleased with us because we are acting like Him. We have become a conduit for His love to the rest of the world. And the more we do this, the brighter we will shine, and others will notice. And hopefully, they will begin to love in the same way.

I should be clear that writing about love and practicing love are two entirely different things. We romanticize love in our society. Boy meets girl, sparks fly, fall in love, and live happily ever after. But that's not the way it works. Love is much more demanding than that. Love is praying for those who hate us. Love is total forgiveness when we've been wronged. These are agonizing and difficult things to do. I have struggled with these things throughout my entire life. But I am getting better at loving others. I am experiencing God's love in so many ways as I give myself more and more to Him. I am much more present to those around me. And I have been able to forgive myself in the process.

Forgiveness is an outgrowth of love and an act of love, whether we are forgiving ourselves or others. But I believe it warrants special attention and so I have devoted the following section to forgiveness.

FORGIVENESS

Forgiveness, as I have already mentioned, is an outgrowth of love. As Christians, we focus on God's forgiveness of our sins. This forgiveness comes as a gift from God through the sacrifice of Jesus. Without this forgiveness, we are lost and at odds with God. Forgiveness is one of the building blocks on which Christianity is founded, and we need to recognize how important it is. "Forgive us our trespasses as we forgive those who trespass against us."[10] In this, the Lord's prayer, we ask to be forgiven the same way we forgive others. So, if we continue holding grudges against people who hurt us, then we can

---

[10] Matthew 6:9-13

expect to be treated in like manner by God. A dire warning indeed.

In my experience, forgiveness has several components which, all taken together, provide a solid framework for how to forgive. Forgiveness can be extremely difficult, particularly when we have been hurt deeply. But there is a way out. Remember, nothing is impossible with God.

Empathy is the capacity to put ourselves in someone else's shoes. It is where all human beings can come together on common ground. When we think of forgiveness, shifting our focus to what the other person is experiencing, is the key. When I find myself needing to forgive another person, I empathize with them and realize that I, too, am a sinner and my actions can hurt another person. There is a spiritual axiom that I learned years ago. "If you are bothered by something someone else is doing, you need look no further than yourself as the cause." We have a choice in how we respond to others. In fact, how we respond to others is the only thing we can control in this world. You may feel angry or hurt, but it's what we do with that anger or hurt that makes all the difference.

Note that I used the word "response" rather than "reaction" here. For me, a "reaction" is an almost instantaneous, primitive force taken with little or no forethought. It is what causes a dog to bite if frightened. By contrast, a "response" requires time and thoughtfulness. We weigh options and we try to understand what the other person is experiencing. We empathize with them. I know from vast experience that if I respond to a situation rather than reacting, I am much more likely to make a good decision. Anyone who has children will be able to empathize.

Empathy also allows me to experience another's suffering. We all suffer, and another's pain might be the very reason they have caused harm. And if we show concern for someone's suffering, we are performing God's work. We are expected to "love our neighbors as we love ourselves."[11]

---

[11] Matthew 26:36-40

Another component of forgiveness is compassion. Having genuine concern for the sufferings or misfortunes of another person is practicing true love. Looking at the person who has harmed us and understanding that we have harmed others in similar fashion, takes the sting out of whatever has happened. When someone comes to me and asks for my forgiveness, all I must do is think of my own sins, my own sufferings, the times I have caused harm, and I become instantly humble. There could be no other response than complete and total forgiveness. It's important to point out here that forgiveness must also be given to people who don't care or might not even know they have harmed us. When Jesus said, "pray for your enemies,"[12] the implication was that they don't necessarily care about our wellbeing.

Some offenses are so evil that only time will bring relief. We may struggle with our entire being to find forgiveness and make seemingly little progress. But our God knows when we are trying. He knows how fragile and weak we

---

[12] Matthew 5:44

are. And if we are making an honest attempt at forgiveness, that we want to forgive, God will bring us the rest of the way. That's been my experience.

Forgiveness also requires prayer. Prayer is perhaps the most important aspect of anything we do in Christian life. Through prayer, we find the strength to forgive, and forgiveness requires great strength. I have heard stories of people finding forgiveness for someone who has killed a loved one. This depth of forgiveness can be found only through prayer and reflection with God. When we pray, we ask for understanding and wisdom. We pray for hope in a world that seems out of control much of the time. And we pray for peace. Peace in the world, and peace in our own lives. We pray for the peace that only Christ can give[13]. A peace beyond anything we can imagine. And once we have been able to forgive people in our own lives, peace is what we find.

---

[13] Philippians 4:7

I think everyone has a story to share when they really had to dig deep to find forgiveness. My own life has not been an easy journey. My life has been difficult. As of this writing, I am experiencing great pain in my life. It feels unbearable at times, and I have often felt hopeless. But my pain brings me closer to Christ. Because of this, I welcome the pain that I experience because I also experience Christ's presence when I feel weak, needy, and hopeless. We are told by Paul to celebrate our weaknesses because it is when we are weak that Christ is most strong[14]. We must get out of the way and let Christ have our pain, disappointments, and turmoil. We, for our part, must be still. And pray. When we do this, we will experience love, forgiveness, hope, faith, light, and joy[15]. And we will find that Christ takes residence in our hearts and minds.

---

[14] 2 Corinthians 12:10
[15] Galatians 5:22

LISTENING TO CHRIST

One of my favorite Christian writers is Louis Evely, a writer and former Catholic priest from Belgium. In his book, "That Man Is You,"[16] he challenges the belief of many modern Christians who think they would have followed Jesus wherever He went if only they had been alive two-thousand years ago. They claim that they would have recognized Jesus and been eager disciples. Louis is not convinced. He argues that we can be every bit as much a disciple today by simply opening the Gospels. There, he says, is where we experience the living Christ.

---

[16] Louis Evely, That Man is You (Paulist Press)

I believe that Christ reveals Himself in the Gospels. And by revealing Himself, He also reveals the Father. The Gospels tell the stories of His ministry. We may have to translate drachmas into dollars, but the stories are rich in content and are as relevant today as they were when the Gospels were first written. The stories that Jesus told so many years ago are about us today. And if we sit quietly and read them, we come to understand why Jesus came into the world. We come to understand His mission. And we come to understand how His message applies to us.

I was asked recently by a family member "what does God look like?" The question took me by surprise because it's just not one you hear every day. I couldn't point to any rendering of Jesus, because I seriously doubt that He was white, tall, gorgeous, with long flowing hair and blue eyes. In fact, the bible disputes this image by inferring just how "regular" Jesus looked. He blended into the community perfectly. I believe that He looked like a regular guy.

This is something that is very important to my faith. Specifically, that Jesus was a man, just like me. He lived and worked in His community, He got tired at the end of the day, He laughed and joked with his friends, He cried when hurt, He got hungry. And He was tempted to sin. Just like me. And yet, He was very different.

One characteristic was Jesus' faith in God. He tells us that "if we have faith the size of a mustard seed, we could move mountains."[17] I pray for more faith every time I sit to offer prayer. And I am very sincere in my request. Yet I keep hearing Jesus asking me "why did you doubt" when I am troubled by something I should be leaving to Him. And I am no different than most people in this regard. Even the Apostles doubted repeatedly. Recall the story when Christ was walking on water towards the Apostles[18]. Peter said, "If it's really you, then bid me to walk toward you." But Peter saw the waves and heard the wind and began to sink because of his lack of faith. Jesus grabbed his hand and asked, "Why did you doubt?".

---

[17] Matthew 17:20
[18] Matthew 14:22-33

And one thing about God is that He will let you take your burdens back if you so choose. He's there to help us carry them. It's us who fail to let God into our lives, not the other way around. He is the incessant knocking at the door[19]. Just how far we can open the door depends on our faith. If we have the faith of a tiny mustard seed, we could open the door completely and for all time. And God wants us to grow in faith, because the Church is strong when its members are strong. And we all make up Christ's body[20]. The Church.

And seeing Jesus' faith in the Gospels, we become aware of the gigantic chasm between His faith and ours. Yet Christ continues to call us to be more like Him. He forgives us, encourages us to be better, strengthens us to go the distance. So, why would anyone push this extraordinary opportunity for true friendship aside? And not just any friend. The Living God. I don't have an answer for that. But I know I have done it many times myself. And Jesus

---

[19] Revelation 3:20
[20] Romans 12:5-6

has been there each time to pick me up and point me toward His path, not mine. Following my own path is what got me into trouble in the first place.

I recall a conversation that I had with my father years ago. I asked him what he would do if he discovered he was not destined for heaven. "I'd argue with God," my father said. I still laugh at his response. My father wasn't serious. He is a devote Christian and a model human being. But while he is a remarkable man, my money's on God winning that argument. But this brings an important point to bear. Don't we argue with God? Haven't we all complained that "the world's just not fair." I do it all the time. But I am getting better at stopping periodically during my day to ask God to keep me on His path. And when I can do that, I am happy.

The Gospels point to Jesus as the one to whom we should be listening[21]. The one to emulate in all we do. And we are challenged to determine "what would Jesus do?" as we

---

[21] Luke 9:35

move throughout our days. John the Baptist tells us that "someone is coming soon who is greater than I am"[22]. And he points to Jesus as the one who will "baptize you with the Holy Spirit and with fire".

Jesus' mother Mary told the people at the wedding in Cana to "do whatever He tells you[23]". And, when they did, they found that He had changed water into wine. And not just any regular wine, but the finest wine according to the head steward of the wedding. "A host always serves the best wine first," he said. "Then, when everyone has had a lot to drink, he brings out the less expensive wine. But you have kept the best until now!"

During Jesus' transfiguration, God the Father says "This is my dearly loved Son, who brings me great joy. Listen to him[24]". We are told that the three Apostles accompanying Him were so terrified that they fell to the ground. But you can surely bet that they listened to Jesus.

---

[22] Mark 1:7
[23] John 2:5
[24] Matthew 17:5-6

And at the last supper, Jesus gave us the eucharist after breaking bread and saying, "This is my body, which is given for you. Do this in remembrance of me. After supper he took another cup of wine and said, this cup is the new covenant between God and his people—an agreement confirmed with my blood, which is poured out as a sacrifice for you."[25] Today, all over the world, people celebrate the eucharist each day in remembrance of Him.

The Gospels also highlight another characteristic of Christ. His toughness. Jesus wasn't afraid of anyone and pointed out hypocrisy and injustice wherever He found it. In fact, the Gospels are filled with instances of this. After He called His first Apostles, the Pharisees and religious leaders asked His disciples why He was eating with such scum[26]. Jesus overheard their question. And He defended them. He came to call sinners to repentance, not the "righteous". And I can imagine His disciples laughing and smiling, knowing that they had this amazing man defending them.

---

[25] Luke 22:19-20
[26] Matthew 9:11

Perhaps the one scene that best defines Jesus' toughness and faith was His agony in the garden of Gethsemane[27]. He knew what was going to happen to Him. He knew He would be betrayed, scourged, and then crucified. He asked the Father three times to save Him from such a brutal death. But by this point in His ministry, Jesus knew His destiny. Everything had been revealed to Him. And so, He went with those who came to arrest Him, accepting his fate.

---

[27] Luke 22:41-44

CALLING THE APOSTLES

When the scribes of the Pharisee party saw him eating with sinners and tax collectors, they said to his disciples, 'Why does he eat with tax collectors and sinners?' When Jesus heard this, he said to them, 'It is not those who are well that need a doctor, but the sick. I have come to call not the righteous, but sinners.'[28]

Are we well or are we sick? Are we among the righteous, or do we eat with other sinners? If we truly want Jesus in our lives, we should gladly identify as being sick sinners. Otherwise, He isn't calling to us.

---

[28] Mark 2:16-17

The Gospels are silent on *how* Jesus called His Apostles. Was there was more conversation between Jesus and His Apostles than just, "Follow me"[29]? No formal introduction? No "who are you, anyway?" Just "follow me." So, either the writers of the Gospels left those conversations out intentionally (which makes no sense), or they simply didn't know enough about them to be included. My bet is that they simply did not know how those conversations went. It was very early in Jesus' ministry. So, we are left to imagine by ourselves. He must have had a charisma that set Him apart, a fearlessness coupled with total acceptance, even for sinners. *Especially* for sinners. Sinners felt comfortable with Him because He accepted them. He came to spread the Good News and He asked these unlikely sinners and tax-collectors to help.

And it's those people who ultimately told His story. And if you think about it, it turns out that this was a very courageous vocation to adopt. It was extremely dangerous to be associated with Christ. The New Testament describes

---

[29] Matthew 4:18-25

the beatings, imprisonments, mistreatments that these men endured. Why would they speak so boldly when their very words could land them in jail with a beating? This has always fascinated me. There's only one good reason they continued to speak out even in the face of such adversity. It was true. Jesus really did come into the world, He really did perform miracles, He really gave us the good news. And He really sacrificed Himself on the cross to blot out our sins. And then He really rose from the dead and ascended into Heaven. It's all true.

Would we have accepted Christ's invitation to drop everything and follow him? It's nice to think that we would, but would we really? Wouldn't we have a few questions for Jesus before making such a decision? What about now? Do we follow Him, hearing His voice calling to us from the Gospels?

None of the Apostles were wealthy or pillars in their communities. In fact, quite the opposite. And they admitted as much. These men had nothing to lose by dropping what they were doing to follow Christ. And they knew they were sinners and not worthy of His calling. But I believe that Jesus chose them precisely because of this. And their journey with Christ was to be something that they couldn't imagine in their wildest dreams.

PEACE WITH DEATH

We are all going to die. It's a part of life. We are conceived, we are born, we live, and then we die. All human beings share this in common. And while our lives can become tangled with various troubles, it's death that frightens us. And the only reason for this is nobody has ever come back from the dead and told the rest of us what it was like. So, we are afraid of the unknown. I think this is a very common reaction to a death. When people die, we have a funeral which is typically a very sad occasion. There are times when someone suffers greatly toward the end of their lives and their deaths can be a relief, particularly for their family and friends.

I lost a baby on the very same day she was born. It was back in 1987 and I was living in New England. She was born prematurely and the tiniest human being I'd ever seen. I could literally hold her inside my outstretched palm. She was named Elizabeth Julianna Babcock. She was born early in the day and died later that night. I will never forget the phone call from the doctor telling me this horrific news. He wanted us to come to the hospital the following day to see her.

When we arrived at the hospital, a nurse brought her to me. I held her and I kissed her tiny forehead. It was ice cold. And that coldness felt colder than any cold I had ever felt. It made me believe that she was dead. I cried very hard. And I wondered about her short life and the purpose of it all. People didn't know what to say. Most people looked at their shoes when I walked into the room. This wasn't supposed to happen. Babies don't die.

Over time, I came to believe that babies do die on occasion, and rather than blaming God for what had happened to me, I found that He was there to comfort me. But it took a long time for me to find peace with what had happened. And I think about her from time to time, wondering what she would have looked like and been like. I know this much; there is no way I could have loved her more than I do. She will forever be my daughter and I look forward to the day when I pass through the "narrow gate"[30] and get to see her face to face.

The good news is that Jesus defeated death for all of us. He died for believers and non-believers alike. He died for everybody. And we all have a chance to find God in our lives. Jesus makes having a relationship with Him easy. He said, "Come to me, all of you who are weary and carry heavy burdens, and I will give you rest. Take my yoke upon you. Let me teach you, because I am humble and gentle at heart, and you will find rest for your souls. For my yoke is easy to bear, and the burden I give you is light."[31] I believe that we all carry heavy burdens, at least during some phase of our lives. Perhaps it is the death of a loved one as in my

---

[30] Matthew 7:13-14
[31] Matthew 11:28-30

case. Or we are having difficulty making ends meet financially. Whatever it is, Christ is there.

My father called me one day and invited me to his induction as a Stephan Minister in his church. I accepted immediately, but had to ask, "What is a Stephan Minister?" He responded by saying "Stephan Ministers help people see how God can solve their problems". My father is a good man and his involvement in the ministry was sure to bring relief with whomever he worked. But I kept playing his response over and over in my thoughts. It wasn't really what he had said. Rather, it was what he did not say. His answer didn't exclude anything. So, God cares about my financial problems? Yes. He cares about all our problems. Financial problems, divorce, loss of a loved one. God cares deeply about you and whatever burdens you happen to be carrying. And there is a simple reason for this. God just wants us to be happy. Joy is one of the fruits of the Holy Spirit.[32] We find joy – real joy – when we surrender ourselves to God's care. We also find love, peace,

---

[32] Galatians 5:22

patience, kindness, generosity, faithfulness, gentleness, and self-control. These all bring happiness.

THE KINGDOM

Jesus tells us that the "Kingdom of God is at hand!"[33] Throughout the Gospels He warns us to be vigilant and ever watchful because we never know when our Savior will come again. It is a warning we should all heed. The simplest way to not get caught off guard is to constantly live by the principles Jesus outlines in the Gospels. Love God with all our heart, all our mind, and all our strength. And to love our neighbor as ourselves. If we do these things we cannot go astray. We will be ready when Christ comes again. And not just that, but this is precisely how we grow th Kingdom of God while living here on Earth.

---

[33] Mark 1:15

When we practice love of God and neighbor, we will not steal from our neighbors, we will be kind to strangers, and our words will be helpful rather than hurtful. Reaching out to strangers can sound a bit dicey what with all the craziness in the world. It takes a leap of faith that God is always with us. That He will guide us and keep us safe. But we must find Christ in those around us. We can find him in the single mother trying to make ends meet for her children. We find him in the tears of someone who has lost a loved one. All it takes to find Christ is looking at the people around us.

But it's not just finding Christ. We must do something. Love is an action verb. It requires that we not only find Christ in those around us, but that we do something to help carry their burdens. We are called to be Simon and help carry one another's crosses[34]. That is true love. Finding Christ in the people around us. We don't have to look very far either. What about the members of our own households? Certainly, there are ample opportunities to

---

[34] Mark 15:21

help our children, spouses, parents, and friends by offering our help.

I had a young man who worked under my supervision many years ago. His personality was abrasive and rude. So much so that none of my other employees even liked the guy. I didn't like the guy. Getting him to do what I wanted was always a struggle. He ate lunch by himself and was clearly a loner. He wound up in the hospital for some testing at one point and I decided to visit him. He enjoyed hunting so I brought along a couple of hunting/outdoor magazines for him to read while confined to his hospital bed. The expression on his face when I walked into the room was one of absolute shock. Other than his mother, I was the only person to visit him during his entire stay. I didn't stay long, but we talked about this and that and he even smiled several times during my short stay. When he returned to work, our relationship was on a totally different footing. He couldn't do enough for me! And we began talking about things that he enjoyed and things that matter. Here was a guy who was rude and difficult who responded to kindness and patience. He responded to love.

Heaven is much closer than we might think. The Holy Spirit lives in our hearts and will guide us if we let Him. Our prayers reach across time and space to God's attentive presence, and He responds by increasing our faith and our ability to love. We simply need to sit still and silent long enough to let Him do His work in us.

When we sit to pray, we don't have to be formal. We need not recite prayers from a prayer book. Although there is nothing wrong with doing so. All we need is a willingness to let God change us. The Gospels tell us that Jesus often went into the countryside to be alone and pray.[35] It is during these times when He came to understand His mission. He tells His Apostles what is going to happen to him on several occasions. That he would be betrayed into the hands of sinners and crucified. While that is not the end of the story, I have often wondered precisely when Jesus truly understood the magnitude of what was going to happen. I believe that his mission was revealed gradually to Him over the three years of His ministry. Every person He

---

[35] Luke 6:12

healed, every miracle He performed, and every time that He knelt to pray brought the story into sharper focus.

THE MINISTRY

Immediately after His baptism by John, we are told that the Holy Spirit descended upon Jesus in the form of a dove.[36] This, I believe, was the beginning of Jesus' ministry. This is when all the pieces started fitting into place. This was also when Jesus was "moved by the Spirit" to wander into the wilderness where He was tempted by Satan.[37] The Gospels of Matthew and Luke provide the most detail about the time Jesus spent in the wilderness. They outline several temptations over a period of forty days, all which Jesus deflected and remained faithful to God. This, I

---

[36] Luke 3:22
[37] Matthew 4:1-22

believe, galvanized Jesus' faith and prepared him for the rest of His journey.

Regardless of which Gospel we start reading, Jesus was met with hostility by the religious leaders of the time. He was tested and questioned. He was accused of breaking the religious laws and customs of the time. He was harassed at every point during his ministry, such was the jealousy of the Pharisees. They were constantly following Jesus to "catch" Him not adhering to some custom or law. They saw Jesus as a threat for two main reasons.

First, Jesus was gaining in popularity and people began to sincerely believe His message and follow Him. This made the Pharisees green with envy, so much so that they were willing to go so far as to kill Him. They watched His every move hoping to catch Him breaking the Sabbath or not following one of their customs. Envy is not a new thing. It was the fuel that drove Jesus' critics mad. And it's the fuel that drives modern-day Pharisees to perpetuate guilt and sorrow. And what did Jesus do to cause such a stir? He gave sight to the blind, He healed the lame, cured those with leprosy, let the deaf hear, raised the dead to life, and preached the Good News to the poor.[38] He did nothing but good. He did nothing but love with a blameless heart, completely and totally. This is what the Pharisees and religious leaders of His time found so troublesome that they plotted to kill Him. And here we are, two-thousand years later and we are still struggling to truly love one another. Still unwilling to forgive those who have wronged us. Driven by fear and lack of understanding.

Second, His message was completely new. The Jews of the time were adhering to the Laws set down by Moses. But Jesus gave the people a brand-new way of looking at God and neighbor. Recall the story from John's Gospel when the towns people dragged a woman who was caught in the very act of adultery to Jesus.[39] "Moses says we should stone such a woman", they jeered. "What do you have to say about this?" Jesus wasn't having it. "Let the one among you without sin be the first to throw a stone". He reminded

---

[38] Luke 7:22
[39] John 8:1-11

them that they are sinners too and that their actions have consequences too. And His message must have stung because they said nothing as they walked away. I imagine it was first time that many of them turned their gaze inward and really took stock of their own spiritual condition. This lesson should not be lost on us either. When was the last time that we dropped the stones that we are holding and took a long, sincere look inside our own souls?

The point of the stories in the Gospels is to make us do just this. Look inside. The Gospel stories are a call to prayer. Every word that Jesus spoke during His ministry was, and still is, a call to prayer. A call to reflect on how our actions impact our relationships with neighbors. And a call to reflect on our relationship with God. The people who dragged that poor woman to Jesus learned a whole new way of looking at sin and struggle. We should too. We all find ourselves doing things that we hate. Even the Apostle Paul said that "I know the difference between right and wrong, but I constantly find myself doing the very things that I despise".[40] I know how that feels. We all do. It's part of the human condition. The good news is that nothing is impossible with God. He hears our prayers and heals us, regardless of our struggles. And that is the essence of grace and forgiveness.

This is what Jesus wants for us. To feel forgiven. To feel accepted. To be listened to. We are very lucky if we have someone in our lives that drops what they are doing just to listen to what we're saying. Sadly, some have nobody. But Jesus has promised that He would never leave us under any circumstances.[41] And he not only hears our voices, but He listens to our very souls. He is in and around us always. His presence is continuous, and He know us better than we know ourselves. So why not talk with Him? Why not share your most intimate prayers with Him? He already knows them. And He would be delighted to sit and listen to us.

I talk with Jesus. I talk with Him in the same way I would talk with a friend. I tell him my problems and those things

---

[40] Romans 7:15
[41] Matthew 28:20

making me anxious. And then, I try to leave them all with Him. The operative word here is "try". God answers our prayers many times in ways that we don't expect. I believe that God actively integrates Himself directly into our lives, at least to the extent that we allow it. We could try to ignore Him, but the fact of the matter would not change that He's still there, loving us, forgiving us even when we don't deserve it.

We never deserve His compassion, yet He's compassionate; we never deserve His forgiveness, yet He's merciful; and we don't deserve His love, yet He loves us. A lot. In fact, Paul tells us that nothing in existence could ever separate us from the love we receive from Christ.[42] Nothing in existence. And His love reflects off us to yet others who continue the chain. Christ's love is limitless, always available to us if only we ask. This is my prayer for you as you read these words… That you realize Christ's love in your life and let His presence guide you.

---

[42] Romans 8:31-39

We learn from the Gospels that at some point in Jesus' ministry, the Apostles asked Him to teach them how to pray.[43] Both Matthew and Luke contain the prayer, yet they are slightly different. In any case, these Gospel verses gave birth to the modern Lord's prayer. We should say it slowly, reflecting on each section.

> *Our Father, who art in heaven, hallowed be thy name;*
> *thy kingdom come; thy will be done on earth as it is in heaven.*
> *Give us this day our daily bread; and forgive us our trespasses*
> *as we forgive those who trespass against us;*
> *and lead us not into temptation, but deliver us from evil.*
> *Amen.*

It is the perfect prayer because it lacks nothing. Everything that we need is covered in this prayer. Seeking God's will, helping us to forgive, keeping us from sin, and even something to eat. This is my go-to prayer when I just want

---

[43] Luke 11:1-10

to be connected. When I stop and say it, I naturally slow down and become aware that I am in the presence of God regardless of where I am. And He is listening to my prayer. Answering my prayer. Answering it in His Own way. This conversation may go on for quite some time too. We just need to keep listening. It's been my experience that we will eventually understand. Of course, there are times when our prayers seem strained and ineffectual. The only answer I know for this is more prayer.

I believe this leads us to pray constantly. This is what God wants. To hear from us constantly, bringing our requests to Him, and letting Him take care of us. Our entire life can become a prayer. Always connected to Christ, letting Him lead us along the path He chooses for us. I love the proverb that says, "Trust in the Lord with all your heart and lean not on your own understanding. In all your ways acknowledge Him, and He will direct your paths".[44] I love it because it is so simple. I love it because it is true.

---

[44] Proverbs 3:5-6

My life has not been easy. I have faced obstacles and challenges throughout my life. And there were many times when I felt totally alone in dealing with them. But nothing could be further from the truth. My relationship with God has evolved. It took me a long time before I finally surrendered to Him. And I have fallen many, many times and needed His mercy and forgiveness. I still fall short and need His constant guidance. But this is not to say that I don't experience joy daily. God's love makes me feel like a pampered child. I am not just tolerated but loved deeply and always near to Him. If I do not feel His presence, it's on me because He is always there, patiently waiting to hear from me.

JESUS AND THE TEN COMMANDMENTS

The Law, otherwise known as the Ten Commandments[45] or the Covenant, was passed by God to Moses on stone tablets. Moses was to deliver the Law to the Israelites waiting at the bottom of the Mount Sinai. It turns out they were badly misbehaving, but this fact departs from the point of my story. God gave people a set of laws by which to live. Don't kill. Don't steal. Don't commit adultery. Most everyone is familiar with at least some of the Commandments. In fact, some of our civil laws reflect the Commandments. For example, we lock up people in our society who kill others. Stealing is considered unlawful.

---

[45] Exodus 20:1-17

These Laws were all that people had before Jesus came into the world. And there were severe penalties for breaking them. Recall the woman caught in the act of adultery.[46] Such women were to be stoned to death for their indiscretion. Very harsh. Paul tells us that, "Yes, people sinned even before the law was given. But it was not counted as sin because there was not yet any law to break".[47]

Jesus respected the Law. He was once asked how to inherit eternal life. And His response was simple and straightforward. Honor your mother and father, don't kill, don't steal. But Jesus came into the world to give us something new. A better way of looking at things. He wants us to view the world through the lens of love. Our response to everything must be loving.

"You must love the Lord your God with all your heart, all your soul, and all your mind. This is the first and greatest commandment. A second is equally important: 'Love your

---

[46] John 8:1-11
[47] Romans 5:13

neighbor as yourself.' The entire law and all the demands of the prophets are based on these two commandments."[48]

This was Jesus' response when asked which was the greatest commandment in the law of Moses. The interesting thing about this response is that nowhere in the Law do these commandments exist. At least not explicitly in the Ten Commandments. And that's because they were new. The Law of Moses was replaced by a new covenant. The old Law was written on stone tablets, but the new Law "…is carved not on tablets of stone, but on human hearts."[49] And the new Law is love.

Everything that Jesus taught and did was based on love. Every miracle, every teaching, every word He spoke had its foundation in love. Instead of not killing our neighbor because it's against the law, we don't kill our neighbor because we express love for them. The law is not even part of the equation. We treat others as we want to be treated. And so rather than remembering all the commandments,

---

[48] Matthew 22:37-40
[49] 2 Corinthians 3:3

we simply love God and our neighbors. At least that is our goal. And Jesus provides ample stories of how to put this love into practice. The parable of the good Samaritan[50] is a wonderful example of how to be a good neighbor. And as you read this story, you will notice that the Law never came into play. Rather, we are told that the Samaritan had compassion on the Jewish traveler. He showed him mercy. And that is, quite simply put, love.

To be clear, I am not suggesting that we ignore the book of Exodus and the Ten Commandments. The stories in the Old Testament are rich in content and are a necessary part of the Christian life. My intention here is to present them in the context of Jesus' ministry and teachings. And this can be a difficult thing to do. Being a light for all people, even those who don't deserve our love and compassion, takes a kind of strength that we can only get from Christ. Only He knows how to love like this. Only He loves without measure and without consideration of our failures. And so, we sit quietly and ask Him to give us that kind of

---

[50] Luke 10:30-37

strength and compassion and love to share with others. By doing so, we become a beacon of God's light to the rest of the world to see.

THE BLESSING OF ADVERSITY

Every morning I read from Sarah Young's "Jesus Calling".[51] One of my dearest friends in the world recommended it. In it, Jesus speaks to us about a myriad of topics. And Sarah provides scripture references as well. It's quite a wonderful book and I highly recommend it. She has written several other related books as well.

One of the things that I have learned from this devotional is that we should thank Jesus for our troubles and struggles. This seemed counter-intuitive at first. Why would I ever be grateful for the troubles in my life? Asking God to help

---

[51] Sarah Young, Jesus Calling (Integrity Publishers)

us with our troubles, sure. But thanking Him? This makes sense for two reasons.

First, overcoming adversity helps us grow, not only as Christians, but as people. Giving thanks should be accompanied by an invitation to God to help us in resolving our adversities. And, if you are like me, there are plenty of opportunities to invite God to help us. Remember, Jesus told us that "Here on earth you will have many trials and sorrows. But take heart, because I have overcome the world."[52] There isn't a single problem with which Jesus cannot help.

The second reason is a bit more complicated. In the second letter to the Corinthians, Paul refers to having a "thorn in the flesh".[53] Whatever it was, it deeply troubled Paul. So much so that he begged God on three separate occasions to take it away. But God refused. He told Paul that "My grace is all you need. My power works best in weakness". So, Paul changed his mind. Instead of complaining about

---

[52] John 16:33
[53] Corinthians 12:1-10

whatever this "thorn" was, he embraced his weaknesses stating that "…when I am weak, then I am strong". To put it another way, we need to get out of God's way and let Him manage our problems. We all have "thorns" in our lives and Christ is telling us to accept them because when we remain weak and out of His way, He does His best work in us.

This is not an easy thing to do. Most of us would say that we can handle the easy problems. We will ask for God's help only when our "thorns" get too sharp. But this is a mistake. We are not qualified to make such determinations. The only option is to give all our concerns, anxieties, fears, complaints, troubles, and problems directly to God. The key is faith. We must believe, or rather *know* that God will give His full attention to whatever concerns us.

And so, adversity can bring us closer to God, to depend on Him more today than yesterday. And to trust that He has our best interest in mind. So, I thank Sarah Young for bringing this to my attention. I now thank God daily for the troubles I will inevitably encounter during each day.

THE ILLUSION OF CONTROL

There is a prayer used by Alcoholics Anonymous[54] called the Serenity Prayer. It goes as follows…

God, grant me the serenity to accept the things I cannot change,
The courage to change the things I can,
And the wisdom to know the difference.

There is more to the prayer than I have included here. It is a beautiful prayer, one that I have recited more times than I can recall. And it took numerous recitations for me to really understand the prayer's message. We all believe that

---

[54] Alcoholics Anonymous, Bill Wilson (AA World Services)

we have some level of control over our own lives. And to a certain extent, I agree. But what can we change? Not much. And everything.

When I say, "not much", I am referring to just about everything that happens in the world. We cannot change the people around us. People have their own thoughts, their own personalities, and their own opinions. And what happens when we force our thoughts and opinions on them? They rebel. And they try to persuade us to behave as they would want. Then, we rebel. If they would just do what we want them to do, everything would be perfect.

So, when we ask God to "grant [us] the serenity to accept the things [we] cannot change", we are referring to everything outside ourselves. We have no control over anything except how we respond to the world. In fact, Alcoholics Anonymous has a spiritual axiom that sums this up perfectly.

"It is a spiritual axiom that every time we are disturbed, no matter what the cause, there is something wrong with us".

And the reason there is something wrong with us is that "us" is all we can change. We only have control over how we respond to what happens to us in daily life. We can choose to accept the things that are happening, or we can choose to rebel against the things that are happening. And this is the reason for the focus on "us".

Many years ago, I decided that I wanted to floss my teeth every night before going to bed. Don't worry, this will make sense in a few more lines. I had read that by flossing our teeth, we can improve our overall health and live longer. Plus, I am married to a dental hygienist. Anyway, for the first few nights I would forget and have to get out of bed and floss. But I was committed to this. So, by the fourth week I had made flossing before bed a habit. A good habit.

The point of this story is to illustrate how difficult it is to change. Does it seem too silly a story? I don't think so. Here was something that could literally add years to my life, and it took me four weeks to make the change permanent. Perhaps this story sounds familiar with something in your life.

Changing the way we think or changing our perspective is difficult. That's why it takes courage to change. We must look closely at ourselves and be willing to admit we are not perfect. I mean, we are perfect at nothing. And when we realize this, we must rally the courage to change. This can be excruciating. And it's important to not get disillusioned or be too hard on ourselves.

I know that I must become more accepting of other people. Yet I find myself being rude and mean to others all too frequently. I know that's not who I want to be. I know that's not who God wants me to be. I am called to be a beacon of light to others, yet so often I fall short. This is a much deeper issue for me than my teeth. But I am willing to do the work and find the man that Christ wants me to be. I am willing to try and overcome long worn-in habits. I am willing, and I believe that willingness is all it really takes. We do our part, and Christ takes us the rest of the way.

So, once we accept our lives as they are, we find serenity. And once we know what we should change, we ask for courage to make the change, and we persevere until we are doing the things that God wants of us. As far as wisdom goes, I believe the Tao te Ching says it best…

Knowing others is intelligence; knowing yourself is true wisdom. Mastering others is strength; mastering yourself is true power.[55]

---

[55] Tao te Ching, Lao-tzu (Translated by Stephen Mitchel, Harper Perennial)

THE LORD'S HANDMAID

Mary said, "Here I am, the Lord's servant. Let it happen to me as you have said. And the angel left her".[56]

This is an incredible scene. The angel Gabriel is sent to Mary with the message that she would bear the son of God. She is alarmed and confused at first. Who wouldn't be? This is unlike any request she'd considered in her young life. And so, it got me wondering whether Mary could have said "no" to Gabriel's incredible announcement. The Gospels provide very little information about Mary prior to the annunciation, so we know very little about her. Even

---

[56] Luke 1:26-28

so, she must have had plans for her life just as any young woman would. We are told that she was betrothed to Joseph. Certainly, she and Joseph must have had plans for their future. Raise livestock, farm, start a family, whatever.

"I'm so very sorry Gabriel, but I have other plans for my life. Surely you can find somebody else who would be willing to do that. Please tell God how much I appreciate Him thinking of me, but I'm not up to the task". This does not sound unreasonable. I pass on requests in my own life when my schedule becomes too cluttered. And I'm sure that she must have had a lot of questions. But instead, Mary said "yes!" and sang the Magnificat. "My soul proclaims the greatness of the Lord…" The depth of Mary's faith was staggering. She accepted God's plan for her life without question or hesitation.

And so, she and Joseph watched Jesus grow up into manhood. They watched Him preach during His ministry, and she experienced the very same feelings that any mother would. She loved Him with all her heart. And then, because of His message to the world, she saw Him scourged and then crucified. This story did not begin and end with Mary and Jesus. Mothers all over the world stand by helplessly while their children are abused, trafficked, killed in drive by shootings, and for no good reason. There are many thousands of mothers who know the pain of cradling their dead children in their arms.

Unlike Mary, for many years I had very little regard for God's will. I struggled to accumulate money, notoriety, material things, status. Not once did it occur to me to ask God what He wanted for my life. In fact, I prayed that God would give me these things. Then I would be happy.

But everything changed one day. I do not remember the date or the circumstances, but these things that I had wanted so badly suddenly seemed so shallow and unnecessary. And so, realizing that these things could not make me happy, I stopped pursuing them, and I turned my attention to finding what God wanted for my life. And, while my mission is not as consequential as Mary's was, I still feel called by God to love, forgive, and accept others just as they are.

So, returning to my initial question of whether Mary could have said "no", I believe that the correct answer is "yes". I believe that Mary could have declined God's request. Otherwise, Mary's response would have been hollow, nothing more than a foregone conclusion. Mary's choice is an example of faith for the rest of us. She believed God and her "yes" brought us our Savior.

And so, I try to meet all of God's requests with the same emphatic "yes" as Mary did. I try and love those around me, help people when the opportunity arises, and make time to communicate with God every day. These are the things that really matter. These are the "yesses" that can change the world.

EMBRACING THE CROSS

By the time Jesus was carrying his cross[57], He had been betrayed, dragged before Pontius Pilot, scourged, mocked, slapped, spat upon, and crowned with thorns. The sight of Him bloodied and disfigured must have been horrifying. And now He is made to carry His cross to the very place He will be crucified. The brutality of His executioners and tormentors is beyond imagining. Jesus endured great pain for our salvation.

What are our crosses? We often hear that someone has a "cross to bear" referring to a specific problem they are dealing with. Perhaps a disability or a difficult living

---

[57] John 19:17-42

condition. Whatever it is, we are asked to bear them just as Jesus did so many years ago. The gospels are timeless.

The Gospels tell the story of a man named Simon of Cyrene [58]who happened to be standing along the route to Jesus' crucifixion. The Romans compelled Simon to carry His cross for him because Christ simply could not carry it on His own. In fact, we are told that Jesus fell three times while carrying His cross, so great was His burden. When He reached Golgotha, He was stripped of His clothes, nailed to the cross, and then He was crucified.

My stepfather died recently. He was a good man who was completely and totally devoted to my mother. He did everything for her. He helped her with her medications, drove her to go shopping, took her on cruises all over the world, and was her best friend. His death left her reeling and feeling absolutely alone. Her burden was crippling, and she stumbled many times.

---

[58] Mark 15:21

My sister and I became Simon, carrying my mother's burden when she could not. Many times, we watched her stumble and fall, and we would pick her up and help her continue carrying her cross, her burden, her grief, her pain. Her pain was palpable and watching my mother go through this left my sister and I totally drained. But we were Simon, and we helped lighten my mother's load.

The work that we are called to do for God is not glamorous. Simon is a case in point. The Romans saw Simon, grabbed him and forced him to carry Christ's cross. Nothing glamorous there. Comforting my mother in light of her husband's death. The same. God's work is not easy. Feeding the hungry, caring for the sick, comforting someone who is in pain are all difficult things to do. But this is God's work. Our willingness to do this sort of work is how we will be judged.

Years ago, I lived in southern New Hampshire. I found a local homeless shelter just over the line in Massachusetts where I volunteered. I did all sorts of work. I cooked meals for the guests, I washed and dried clothing (much of which were children's clothing), I made lunches, and I did whatever was necessary during my appointed work slots.

One night I was working the after-dinner shift washing, drying, and folding clothes and making lunches. This shift ran from 8 PM through midnight. Working with another volunteer, it seemed as if we made a thousand lunches that evening. But I knew that each one would be eaten and appreciated by someone in need.

Another time I had been assigned to the dinner shift. The dinner shift was a big deal because it required cooking for at least thirty people, something I never mastered. Well, on this occasion, I was the only volunteer who showed up for the dinner shift. But I was determined to get the job done and started looking through the pantry and refrigerator for what I would cook. But the task seemed daunting, and it crossed my mind more than once to sneak out and go home. But I stayed and started planning my menu. While my head was spinning with my menu planning, the most amazing thing occurred. The front door of the shelter opened, and fifteen nuns filed into the large kitchen. Their whale-watching excursion had been cancelled and so they decided to see how they could help at the shelter. I was shocked as the nuns asked me what they could do to help. Before I knew it, the aroma of cooking food filled the kitchen and dinner was served to thirty grateful (and hungry) guests. Before I knew it, my shift was finished, and I received hugs from each nun before walking to my car.

Now, it could have been sheer coincidence that the whale watching excursion was rained out and these particular nuns arrived to help, but I somehow feel that God played a part in this. God saw my struggles and sent not just one, but fifteen Simons to help carry my load.

THE PRODIGAL SON

When we read the story of the prodigal son[59], with whom do we most identify? It's not surprising that we most often identify with the prodigal son. Like him, we are often disobedient and in need of God's forgiveness. But what about the father? What about the second son? Can we relate to them as well?

The son has just asked his father for his share of his father's inheritance. He thought nothing of how rude his request had been to start with. He couldn't even wait for his father's death! He just wanted his share of the money. His

---

[59] Luke 15:11-32

selfishness is staggering. But the father acquiesced and gave his son his inheritance.

So, the son packs his things, puts the money in his pocket, and off he goes to distant lands to find fame and fortune. But rather than acting responsibly, he squanders his inheritance on prostitutes, liquor, and whatever else we might consider. Certainly not the outcome the father had planned for his son.

The whole thing goes sideways on him, and he finds himself broke, tired, and hungry. After considerable thought (and hunger), he decides to head back home and ask for forgiveness. He even composes a little confession speech asking only to be treated as one of his Father's servants. At least they were eating well. So, with hat in hand, he begins the journey back to his father.

What would we say to our returning son? After all, this mess is of his own doing. "I figured you'd be back at some point", we might say. "I am very disappointed in you. Go get cleaned up and we will talk about this later. I hope you've learned your lesson". This seems appropriate under the circumstances. After all, his son's behavior has been nothing short of despicable.

But that's not what happens.

The father is watching for his son's return, anticipating the moment they are reunited. Perhaps the father knew all along that his son would return. Perhaps he had done something similar in his youth.

We are told that the father sees the son returning from a distance and runs out to greet him. When he reaches his son, the son recites his pathetic apology, begging to be allowed to stay even if only as a servant. The father completely ignores the son's apology and requests a robe for his son as well as a ring for his finger. Then he says, "my son was dead and has come back to life".

It's probably evident that the father in this story represents God the Father. We are the prodigal son. But there's another character in this story. The father's "good" son who obeyed his father throughout his brother's ordeal. He is shocked to find that his brother, after everything he's done, has been forgiven by his father.

The truth is, we play all three roles at different times in our lives. Haven't we been the prodigal son, in need of forgiveness by someone we've hurt? Haven't we forgiven someone who has hurt us with no strings attached? And haven't we been the "good" son complaining that someone is not being punished appropriately for their crimes?

I believe this is a story for everyone simply because we can all identify with each role in this story. But the focus is obviously on forgiveness. How do we forgive? Begrudgingly, or eagerly? Completely, or with strings attached?

The Father forgives his son. He forgives him completely and absolutely without even a hint of reprisal. His forgiveness is so pure that it demands absolute humility. We may even find it shocking. He doesn't even listen to his son's confession. There was no need to; he had forgiven the boy while he was still a long way off.

THE LOVE OF CHRIST

"For I am convinced that neither death nor life, nor angels, nor rulers, nothing already in existence and nothing still to come, nor any power, nor height nor depths, nor any other created thing will be able to separate us from the love of God in Christ Jesus our Lord".[60]

If we do not find comfort in this passage, we should repeatedly read it until we do. It should become a mantra, endlessly repeating itself to bring us reassurance, strength, and confidence. A reminder that Christ is in control, and nothing can change that reality.

---

[60] Rom 8:37-39

But this takes time, like most things of value. When I was a younger man, I thought my sins were so abhorrent that they somehow disqualified me from receiving this promise. I spent so much time tallying and confessing my sins that I felt no joy at all. And since joy is a fruit of the Spirit, it appeared that I had none of God's Spirit. I was miserable. So much so that I felt unsure of whether I was destined for Heaven. Hell seemed more like it, but I still I held out hope. And I am sure glad that I did. My relationship with God is growing ever deeper with each time I acknowledge my need for Him. And each time I whisper His name inviting Him to take my life and mold me into whatever He wants me to be.

And I must be ready to see whatever Christ shows me, because whenever we look deeply into ourselves, we will see things that we may not particularly like. It takes strength to make this inward journey. But we will also see the good things in our lives. Why do we believe that He cares more about the ugly than the good in us? The Lord corrects me where He sees fit, but I always know that He loves me.

And so, it turns out that my sins are nothing compared to God's love for me. He loves me, not despite my faults, but with my faults. Parents understand this completely. We love and help our children as they struggle through life remembering that we went through the very same trials, the very same heartaches, and made the very same mistakes. And though they often rebel against us, we love them with every ounce of our being. A perfect reflection of God's love for us.

The following three sections are from a book entitled the Tao te Ching[61]. The title can be translated as "The Book of the Way". It is a Chinese classic written by a gentleman named Lao-tzu around the date 400 BC.

As I indicate below, the book espouses many of the same values as Christianity. As such, I feel compelled to include a small sampling of Lao-tzu's masterpiece with my other writings. It is a book well-worth reading. I hope you enjoy it!

---

[61] Tao te Ching, Lao-tzu (Translated by Stephen Mitchel, Harper Perennial)

A good traveler has no fixed plans and is not intent upon arriving.
Tao de Ching, 27

I like this statement from the Tao. I interpret this saying as "the journey IS the goal". Our lives can be littered with any number of goals, each demanding our attention and energy. Now, I understand that reaching goals is not a bad thing. We need them in our lives. Without goals we would never learn to play guitar, create beautiful jewelry, catch a softball, or take a pretty photograph.

But what about the time and effort spent in reaching these goals? Without it, we would never reach them. So, it seems that the journey from now to achieving a specific goal is in many ways more important than actually reaching the goal. Much more so.

But the world we live in couldn't care less about the journey. Take this pill and lose 20 pounds in 30 days, guaranteed! Use our muscle gizmo machine for five minutes a day and look like this perfect male specimen! Learn to play guitar like a rock star with our newly updated videos for just X dollars with free shipping for a limited time. We want results now. There's no time to "waste" working toward a goal. The goal must come now.

I love hiking. My wife and I visit a park near our house that has many hiking trails and depending on how much time we have determines the length of the trail we choose for that day. But regardless of which trail we choose; we wind up right back where we started. The "goal" of the hike is the hike itself.

I have also been on hikes where we've gotten lost. There was one hike we started that was about six miles long. At about mile thirteen, we came across a park ranger who laughed and told us just how far off the trail we had gotten. We weren't even close. But he was kind enough to drive my wife and I, along with our dog, back to our campsite. So, when you start a journey, enjoy each and every moment of it. And be ready for unexpected detours.

**The Tao doesn't take sides.
It gives birth to both good and evil.
The Master doesn't take sides.
She welcomes both saints and sinners.**

Tao Te Ching, 5

The Tao, while not Christian scripture, espouses many Christian ideals. This section of chapter 5 is a great example. "...for he causes his sun to rise on the evil as well as the good, and he sends down rain on the righteous and the wicked alike", Matthew 5:45. If this is how God acts toward both the good and no-so-good, shouldn't we do the same? It's not our job to determine who's good and who's evil anyway. That determination should be made by God alone.

Judging someone - their actions, thoughts, political views - is dicey business. For starters, we don't really know what's going on in someone else's head. We really don't know what motivates people. And it feels unfair when someone else does it to us. Really unfair.

The only person who is qualified and intimate enough to do this is Jesus. He's with us all the time. He knows our every thought, knows precisely what motivates us, and - this is only my opinion - wishes we would stop moving long enough to get to know Him better. He wants that. "I stand at the door and knock…". The question at hand is whether or not we open it for Him.

And it is somewhat understandable why many people hesitate to open the door. Loving is difficult business. It demands that we love even those who hate us. It demands that we are patient and kind. And not to just people we like, but also with those we don't. But opening the door also gives us Christ and His moment by moment presence, His care and protection. His completely unconditional love. Open the door and see.

Do you have the patience to wait till your mind settles and the water is clear?

Tao Te Ching, 15

Anyone who has stirred mud into a glass of clear water knows exactly what happens. The mud mixes with the water and moves in a circular motion from the bottom to the top of the glass. Gradually, over time, the circular motion slows, and the mud begins settling at the bottom of the glass. But if we watch closely, it takes quite a while before every speck of mud settles.

The chaos and clutter of our days are the same. We wake up and immediately begin stirring the mud in our glasses. It rises, overtaking any clarity, and before we even drink our first coffee, our days are filled with the usual madness of working, parenting, cooking, cleaning, driving, etc. It's little wonder that the mud rises right up to the very top of the glass. And with everything we do, we keep the whirlpool moving around and around.

I used to believe that doing nothing was a waste of time. Just think of how much more productive it is to be doing something. But being still is not a waste of time and it could be some of the most productive time spent during a busy day. At least this has been my experience. Taking a few moments to ask God for strength throughout the day is not doing nothing. It's communicating with the one Person who can really help us. It's fostering the one relationship where patience, kindness, joy, and pardon are always available.

When the COVID pandemic hit the US, like most people, I was forced to work from home. At first, I hated it. I much preferred working in the office as it was stimulating, and I enjoyed sharing ideas with my teammates. But the pandemic continued with no end in sight.

So, I decided that I needed to change my mind and embrace the slower pace and quiet that the pandemic brought to my work. I found that I actually needed and appreciated the new pace, the quiet of each day. I was still busy with work, but everything around it was still. And for the first time in a long time, my mud settled, and I could see more clearly. It is only in the quiet that we can hear God's voice.

FINDING CHRIST

There are a lot of people who do not believe in God because, they say, there is no evidence for such a belief. Or perhaps they've had a difficult life and cannot believe in a God who appears so unfair, so uncaring. A quick look at the evening news and it's easy to conclude that the world is spiraling out of control. Where is God in all of this? Why doesn't He intervene and bring peace to the world? If God really loved us, there would be no hunger, no sickness, no wars. I could go on. But finding Christ is not an exercise in intelligence. It is an exercise in faith.

Years ago, I met a man who organized a support group specifically for people who had lost children. Some of the children died of sickness, some died of an accident. His child died when he backed over her moving his car out of the garage. She was only two years old. And it was Christmas morning. It was, by anyone's accounting, an absolute disaster.

As I sat with this man and listened to him share this story, I was amazed to find how deeply he trusted that God would get him through this. There was no questioning God's presence in his life, so firmly ingrained was this man's faith. I sat in awe as he told me how God got him through this awful time in his life. I was edified by his faith. And I carry his story in my heart to this very day.

I would hope that most of us will never have to endure such misfortune. Unfortunately, some of us will, and our faith will be tested. How will we respond? It depends on our relationship with God.

Finding Christ is simple. And it's also extremely difficult. Finding Christ is simple because He is always available to us. He wants us to call out to him when we are in pain. He wants us to believe that He can help us. All we must do is ask. Where this becomes difficult is when we have expectations of what our relationship with God should look like.

I believe that I have found Christ and that He is active in my life. I found Him by sitting quietly and feeling His presence. I read scripture and try to apply it in my life. And then I sit quietly some more. In my experience God's voice can be heard only when there are no other distractions. Compared to the world in which we live, God's voice is a quiet whisper. But I assure you, if you listen with your heart, you will hear Him speaking to you. And you will be changed forever.

www.ingramcontent.com/pod-product-compliance
Lightning Source LLC
Chambersburg PA
CBHW061801070526
44586CB00023B/2660